CONTEMPORARY BIOGRAPHIES

CAITLIN CLARK

by Libby Wilson

BrightPoint Press

San Diego, CA

BrightPoint Press

an imprint of ReferencePoint Press, Inc.
Printed in the United States

For more information, contact:
BrightPoint Press
PO Box 27779
San Diego, CA 92198
www.BrightPointPress.com

LIBRARY OF CONGRESS CATALOGING-IN-PUBLICATION DATA

Names: Wilson, Libby (Freelance writer), author.
Title: Caitlin Clark / by Libby Wilson.
Description: San Diego, CA: BrightPoint Press, [2026] | Series: Contemporary biographies | Includes bibliographical references and index. | Audience: Grades 7–9
Identifiers: LCCN 2024055870 (print) | LCCN 2024055871 (eBook) | ISBN 9781678211509 (hardcover) | ISBN 9781678211516 (eBook)
Subjects: LCSH: Clark, Caitlin, 2002---Biography--Juvenile literature. | Women basketball players--United States--Biography--Juvenile literature. | Basketball players--United States --Biography--Juvenile literature.
Classification: LCC GV884.C554 .W55 2026 (print) | LCC GV884.C554 (eBook) | DDC 796.323092 [B]--dc23/eng/20250116
LC record available at https://lccn.loc.gov/2024055870
LC eBook record available at https://lccn.loc.gov/2024055871

CONTENTS

AT A GLANCE

- Caitlin Clark was born on January 22, 2002, in West Des Moines, Iowa.

- From age 5, Caitlin had excellent shooting and ball-handling skills, as well as the ability to see what was happening on the court.

- In high school, Caitlin hit thirteen three-pointers and scored sixty points in one game. She was the Gatorade Player of the Year 2 years in a row.

- Clark led the University of Iowa Hawkeyes to two NCAA National Championship Games. 23 million people watched the games on TV.

- On March 3, 2024, Clark broke the all-time NCAA scoring record. Clark graduated with 3,951 points, the most ever scored by any college player, male or female.

- Clark earned assists on almost 50 percent of the Hawkeyes' baskets. She became the first woman to lead NCAA Division I in both scoring and assists in the same season.

- In April 2024, Clark was drafted by the WNBA's Indiana Fever. As a rookie, Clark led them to the WNBA playoffs.

- Clark's huge national fan base followed her from college into the WNBA, leading to attendance and TV viewership records.

A RECORD-SETTING SHOT

Excitement rolls through Carver-Hawkeye Arena. Fans have traveled hundreds of miles to be part of basketball history. Caitlin Clark plays for the University of Iowa Hawkeyes. On this night, the 22-year-old will break the National Collegiate Athletics Association (NCAA) women's scoring record. It stands at 3,527 points. Clark needs just eight points to pass it.

Two weeks after breaking the women's NCAA scoring record, Caitlin Clark scored the 3,685th point of her college career to become the NCAA's all-time leading scorer for men or women.

IOWA
22

The Iowa women's basketball team celebrates Clark's record-breaking moment with a team photo.

It doesn't take long. Clark scores five points in the first minute of the game. It's her third shot that makes history. On a fast break, Clark pulls up near the center court logo and lets the ball fly. It soars 35 feet (10.7 m) and falls into the basket with a *swish*! Now Clark has scored more points than any other woman in NCAA history. The crowd cheers.

Clark repeatedly launches shots that fly like missiles from impossible distances straight into the hoop. The crowd roars in amazement. Few understand how much practice it takes for Clark to make her shots look easy.

After the game, Clark thanks her parents, coaches, and fans. She points to her teammates. "This wouldn't be possible if it wasn't for these girls," Clark says.[1]

THE CAITLIN CLARK EFFECT

Clark is transforming women's basketball. As a **point guard**, Clark pushes the game to a fast and furious pace. Her pinpoint passes help her teammates rack up points.

Playing for the WNBA had always been a goal for Clark.

And those behind-the-back and no-look passes electrify audiences.

Clark built a huge national fan base during her four college seasons. In 2024, many fans followed her to the Women's National Basketball Association (WNBA). These fans are smashing attendance records. Games are moving to larger arenas. Television ratings are skyrocketing. Clark is inspiring millions of people to love women's basketball as much as she does.

CHAPTER ONE

RIGHT FROM THE START

Caitlin Clark was 4 years old when she watched her dad take off her older brother's bicycle training wheels. She became upset. If 6-year-old Blake could do it, why couldn't she? Caitlin insisted that her training wheels come off, too. So her dad took them off, and she rode away as if she'd been doing it all her life. At an early age, Caitlin was already competitive, confident, and coordinated.

As a teenager, Caitlin Clark had opportunities to play with youth national teams through USA Basketball.

USA
172
molten

Caitlin's top-notch passing skills may have been honed on the soccer field. She played varsity soccer at Dowling Catholic as a freshman and sophomore.

Caitlin was born on January 22, 2002, to Brent Clark and Anne Nizzi-Clark. Caitlin and her brothers grew up in West Des Moines, Iowa. They played basketball all the time with their cousins, most of whom were boys. The boys let Caitlin play. But they didn't take it easy on her. Caitlin struggled to keep up. Sometimes she would run into the house crying. Her parents told her if she wanted to play, she had to learn to hold her own.

Through sixth grade, Caitlin always played on boys' teams. She even played up a year, so the boys she played were older. Caitlin loved the challenge.

FAMILY OF ATHLETES

Family life for the Clarks revolved around sports. Both her parents had grown up around sports. Caitlin's dad had played basketball and baseball at Simpson College in Iowa. Her brother Blake was a quarterback for the Iowa State University football team. Caitlin's younger brother,

Colin, played several sports at Dowling Catholic High School. The family liked to compete. They believed in working hard to do their best.

Early on, Caitlin had special skills. "I don't recall that she would ever miss a shot," Brent Clark said. "The baskets were at 5 or 6 feet [1.5 or 1.8 m]. She would just pull up from the free-throw line and swish."[2]

Young Caitlin also had a good understanding of the game. She could analyze what was happening on the court. She could react quickly and be ready for what was going to happen next.

Right from the start, Caitlin played with great emotion. Her joys and frustrations were plain to see. She cried after every game her team lost. "That's because of how much I cared. I'm like 6 years old, and it didn't matter, obviously. But it mattered to me," Caitlin said.[3] She remembers being kicked out of gym class in third grade for being too competitive.

Growing up, Caitlin participated in many activities. She tried basketball, soccer, volleyball, softball, tennis, and piano. Caitlin was an All-State soccer player by her sophomore year of high school. But her heart demanded basketball. In third

Meeting Maya Moore

When Caitlin was about 10, she met Maya Moore of the WNBA's Minnesota Lynx. Moore was Caitlin's idol. It meant the world to Caitlin, so now she makes a point to sign autographs and take photos with fans at every game.

grade, Caitlin was assigned to write down her dreams. Her number-one dream was to play in the WNBA.

HIGH SCHOOL SHOOTING STAR

Caitlin played 4 years of basketball for Dowling Catholic High School in West Des Moines. Coach Kristin Meyer first saw Caitlin playing in an eighth-grade tournament. Meyer was amazed by the point guard's ability to see plays unfold and react quickly. Caitlin's shooting and passing were also next level. But her confidence and fearlessness impressed Meyer most.

Caitlin's biggest challenge was controlling her emotions. When a teammate made a mistake, Caitlin would throw up her arms in disgust or get angry. She made

Caitlin Clark stepped into the national spotlight as a sixth grader when she began playing for the All Iowa Attack, a well-respected basketball academy.

everyone nervous. Caitlin felt alone. Her teammates just played for fun. When the team lost, they didn't care as much as she did.

Meyer began showing Caitlin film clips of her outbursts on the court. It helped Caitlin to see herself as others did. Meyer benched Caitlin as needed to remind her to keep her emotions under control.

Caitlin Clark's ability to score three-point shots captured the attention of college scouts.

One summer, Caitlin failed to make a youth international team. It stung. The year before, Caitlin had won a gold medal in international play. Caitlin was determined not to get cut again. She worked harder. Caitlin made the international team the following year and won another gold medal.

By her senior year, Caitlin had become nationally known. In one game, she scored sixty points. She hit thirteen three-pointers, breaking the state's three-point record. When the game ended, students lined up to get Caitlin's autograph, just like in the pros.

Caitlin averaged more than thirty points per game during her senior year. She twice became the Gatorade Player of the Year. Caitlin was chosen as Miss Iowa Basketball, too.

Nearly every college in America wanted to **recruit** Caitlin. She chose to play for the University of Iowa. It was nearby, so her family could attend games. Caitlin meshed well with Coach Lisa Bluder and her team. Plus, the Hawkeyes' point guard was graduating. Caitlin would have an opportunity to play immediately.

The NCAA Final Four is the semifinals of the national championship tournament. The Hawkeyes had last reached the Final Four 30 years ago. Caitlin's goal was to lead them back. Though Iowa had a solid women's basketball program, it wasn't ranked among the top teams in the country. Many people thought Caitlin's goal was a long shot. But then, long shots were Caitlin's specialty.

Caitlin briefly accepted an offer from Notre Dame before ultimately deciding to play for the Iowa Hawkeyes.

CHAPTER TWO

IOWA HAWKEYE

At Iowa, Clark had a tight-knit group of friends for the first time. "What she found is people who also put their entire life into basketball," teammate Kate Martin said.[4] Clark felt free to act natural and have fun. She would hit a half-court shot to end practice. Then she'd whip off her shirt and whirl it above her head while running through the bleachers. "When she's like that, everybody laughs," Coach Bluder said.

Through basketball at the University of Iowa, Caitlin Clark connected with teammates who shared her drive and goals.

"The season is stressful. You need somebody that's willing to be goofy and fun."[5]

THE MAKING OF A LEADER

Clark recorded 27 points and 8 rebounds in her first college game. She continued working hard on her skills. Bluder often saw her working on her shot in the practice gym. Clark also lifted weights to improve her **conditioning**.

Clark's temper still flared when she got frustrated. She might throw a water bottle or slam a chair. Handling her emotions was Clark's biggest challenge. As Meyer had done, Bluder showed Clark film clips of her outbursts. Bluder also brought in a **sports psychologist** to work with the team.

Bluder coached Clark on leadership skills. Clark learned to take the blame when teammates fumbled her passes. Martin advised Clark to meet her teammates

Iowa coach Lisa Bluder checks in with Clark on the sidelines during a game against the Colorado Buffaloes.

at their own levels. Over time, Clark's emotional control improved. During a nationally televised game, Clark made just one of thirteen shots from the three-point line. Afterward, Clark simply hit the gym and practiced her shot.

The Hawkeyes ranked sixth in their conference during Clark's freshman year. They ranked first the next year. As a sophomore, Clark became the first woman to lead the NCAA Division I in both scoring and **assists**. This showed Clark was not a selfish shooter. She didn't focus only on her scoring record. Clark passed often, helping her teammates score. Clark was chosen for many first team All-American honors. Twice she won the Dawn Staley Award for the best point guard in the country.

NATIONAL STAR

Clark's skills expanded in college. Her threes became logo threes. She often scored triple-doubles. A triple-double is when a player earns double digits in three of five categories. The categories are points, assists, steals, blocks, and rebounds. Clark's pinpoint passes dazzled fans. So did her full-court passes. Clark accurately threw the ball to where a teammate was heading. Martin said it was like Clark could

How Far Does Clark Shoot?

The NCAA three-point line is 22 feet 1.75 inches (6.75 m) from the basket's center. But Clark often shoots from even farther away. These "logo shots" are 25 to 30 feet (7.6 to 9.1 m) away. Clark shoots 39.2 percent from this zone.

see the future on the basketball court. Clark earned assists on almost 50 percent of Hawkeye baskets.

Clark's fame skyrocketed during her junior year. Her logo shots and on-court wizardry attracted new viewers to women's basketball. Mobs of screaming fans gathered outside of arenas to welcome the Hawkeyes. Clark's fans spent $52 million in 1 year on hotels, food, and gas. People called this economy boost "Clarkonomics."

MARCH MADNESS

Clark's goal for her team was to reach the Final Four. This is part of the yearly NCAA national championship tournament. Each March, top teams in the nation compete until only four teams remain unbeaten.

These four teams play in the Final Four. The winners play each other in the NCAA Championship Game. Iowa hadn't been to the Final Four since 1993.

Clark took possession of the ball during the final minutes of the 2024 NCAA championship game against the South Carolina Gamecocks.

The Hawkeyes made the Final Four in 2023. It was an action-packed game. Iowa beat the undefeated South Carolina Gamecocks 77–73. Clark scored forty-one points. The game drew better TV ratings on ESPN than any regular-season National Basketball Association (NBA) game ever shown on the network.

The Hawkeyes advanced to Iowa's first NCAA Championship Game. They lost to Louisiana State University 102–85. The Iowa players were brokenhearted. They vowed to make the championships again in 2024.

In her senior year, Clark led Iowa through another successful season. Along the way, Clark made headlines. She broke the NCAA women's scoring record in a game against Ohio State on February 15, 2024.

CAITLIN CLARK'S COLLEGE STATISTICS

Year	Games	Points per Game	Total Points	Assists	Steals	Turnovers	Free Throw Percentage
2020–2021	30	26.6	799	214	38	144	85.8
2021–2022	32	27.0	863	257	47	152	88.1
2022–2023	38	27.8	1,055	327	57	158	83.9
2023–2024	39	31.6	1,234	346	68	185	86

Source: "Caitlin Clark," Men's and Women's College Basketball Statistics and History, *n.d. www.sports-reference.com.*

Clark scored 3,951 points in college, more than any other player in NCAA history, male or female.

Two weeks later, Clark broke the NCAA all-time scoring record. She had scored more points in college than any player in history.

The excitement carried the Hawkeyes into the 2024 national championship tournament. Clark led the Hawkeyes to the title game. Yet once again they fell just short. They lost to South Carolina in the last game of the season.

Clark had many accomplishments in her college career, including becoming the all-time leader in points among women's college basketball players.

AN IMPORTANT CHOICE

During Clark's senior year, she faced a major decision. The COVID-19 pandemic had shortened some NCAA seasons in 2020. Some players were allowed to play for a fifth year. Clark had to decide if she should stay at college or move to the WNBA.

A debate played out in the media. Some said Clark would do well in the WNBA. She might be an All-Star her first season. Others said Clark wasn't physical enough to play pro. Sports fans looked forward to seeing what was next for Clark.

CHAPTER THREE

A DREAM COME TRUE

Clark always steps up to a challenge. She knew the WNBA would be a big step up. A **rookie** doesn't get to choose their WNBA team. Instead, they are entered into a lottery. The lowest-ranked teams have the highest odds of getting the best new players.

The Indiana Fever had the highest odds in 2024. The team had won just eighteen games in 2 years. The Fever won the first

Caitlin Clark dribbles down the court in search of a teammate to pass to during the September 19, 2024 game against the Washington Mystics.

Lilly
INDIANA
22
Wilson

draft pick. Of course, the team drafted Clark. Fever fans hoped Clark's skills would raise the team's standing.

But it wasn't going to be easy. Clark was coming into a team that hadn't been very successful. And the Fever faced a brutal opening schedule. The team played eleven games in 20 days against strong teams. The Fever had little time to practice. Still, the team set a goal of making the playoffs.

Having to play without much rest made Clark's adjustment to the WNBA difficult. Rookies already have no break between college and their pro season. Clark couldn't even attend her college graduation. Players finish college courses and do media appearances. Most have to move to a new city and find housing.

Clark scores a layup against Cameron Brink, helping Indiana win 78–73 against the Los Angeles Sparks in May 2024.

TOUGH START

The Fever got off to a rough start in the 2024 WNBA season. After eleven games, the Fever had two wins and nine losses. Two of the losses were blowouts.

But Clark's individual statistics were great. She led all 2024 rookies in scoring, three-pointers, and assists. The WNBA named her May's Rookie of the Month. Still, some Fever fans were disappointed. They were upset that Clark hadn't immediately turned the Fever into a powerhouse. Clark felt pressured. She took care of her mental health. For Clark, that meant asking for help. It also meant telling people when she was struggling.

Clark and her teammates tried to ignore the critics, especially those on social media.

Clark takes the ball up the court during a playoff game against the Connecticut Sun on September 25, 2024.

For Clark, blocking criticism was necessary. She loved playing basketball. She didn't want the meanness to affect her feelings for the game.

Many people thought Clark should be on that summer's US Olympic basketball team. Playing in the Olympics had long been a dream of hers. However, the coaches ultimately decided to leave Clark off the team.

Clark remained positive. She said, "I'm going to be rooting them on to win gold."[6] Clark also said it gave her something to work for. She hoped to make the next Olympic team.

Though Clark was left off the Olympic team, she was chosen for the WNBA All-Star team. The All-Star team played the

Record-Breaking Fans

Clark's record-breaking season attracted a record number of fans. ESPN reported WNBA viewership was up 170 percent over 2023 and that WNBA ratings had soared. Attendance at 2024 Fever home games surpassed 300,000 after nineteen games. This set another new WNBA record.

Olympic team as a practice game before the Olympics. Clark, Arike Ogunbowale, and Angel Reese led the All-Star team. The All-Stars beat the Olympians 117–109.

THE FEVER CATCH FIRE

The Fever used the month-long Olympic break for some much-needed practice. The teammates became comfortable playing together. Coach Christie Sides empowered Clark to become the voice of the team. After the break, Clark called the plays. She became the team's leader on the court.

The Fever played the Phoenix Mercury right after the break. Phoenix had three Olympic players, but the Fever beat them 98–89. Then the Fever found their groove, winning eight of their next ten games.

The Fever ended the season with twenty wins and twenty losses. They clinched the sixth seed for the WNBA playoffs. The players were thrilled to make the playoffs. But their season ended in the first round with a close loss to the Connecticut Sun.

Clark walked away from the 2024 season with the WNBA Rookie of the Year trophy, edging out long-time rival Angel Reese of the Chicago Sky.

Clark was disappointed with the loss but felt she'd had a solid first season. In fact, Clark had been a record-breaking rookie. She broke the WNBA rookie scoring record with 769 points. Clark's 337 assists set a WNBA single-season record. Clark led the league in logo shots. Clark was the obvious choice for WNBA Rookie of the Year. She was also voted onto the All-WNBA First Team. Yet, Clark said she has a lot of room for improvement. She felt she had just scratched the surface.

CHAPTER FOUR

MORE THAN BASKETBALL

When not playing basketball, Clark spends most of her time with family and friends. She's part of a large Italian-American family. Clark is one of twenty grandchildren on her mom's side. Clark's extended family has been a big part of her life and success.

Clark has a great relationship with her parents. Clark says, "My mom is somebody I talk to every single day. My life would be

Clark's family has supported her throughout her career, from her father's coaching when she was young to her mother's business guidance.

This was never a long shot.
IOWA
22

a mess if it weren't for her. She's one of my best friends."[7] Clark's dad has always been a constant in her life. Clark's parents attended all her college games.

Clark is also very close to her brothers. She was inspired by her brother Blake's efforts in high school football. He was very athletic. But he was not the most skilled player. Blake worked harder than everyone else to succeed. Clark and her brother Colin adore each other. The three siblings stay in touch.

DOWNTIME

In her off-hours, Clark spends time with her boyfriend, Connor McCaffery. They began dating in April 2023. McCaffery played basketball at the University of Iowa.

Clark and McCaffery attend sporting events together and find time to relax.

His dad was Iowa's head coach. In 2024, McCaffery became an assistant men's basketball coach at Butler University in Indianapolis. McCaffery and Clark practice basketball together. He is supportive during tough times.

Clark likes to unwind on the golf course as well. She plays about four times a week during her off-season. Golf is something calm Clark can do outside with the people she loves. In 2023, she played in a tournament with golf pro and fellow Iowan Zach Johnson.

Another of Clark's hobbies is baking. She and her mom enjoy spending time in the kitchen time together. Clark especially likes making brownies.

BUSINESSWOMAN

Clark enrolled in the University of Iowa without declaring a major. But she found her calling in a marketing class. A marketing professor brought in former students who now worked at Amazon and Microsoft.

For Clark, golf provides a way to relax and spend time outdoors.

They participated in a problem-solving exercise that Clark found engaging. Clark graduated as an honors student in marketing.

Marketing was the perfect major for Clark. As of 2021, NCAA athletes were allowed to be paid for ads using their name, image, and likeness (NIL). Many businesses wanted to sign Clark. Several **agents** reached out to represent her. But the Clark family wasn't sure whom to trust.

Clark's mom was a marketing professional. She and other family members studied NIL. They helped Clark set up a company to represent her interests. Its name is CC28 Ventures, LLC. Her mom is head of its strategic partnerships. Clark signed deals with Gatorade, Nike, State

Clark signed a contract to endorse Gatorade in 2023, becoming only the second women's basketball player to do so.

Farm, and others. Her ads helped make Caitlin Clark a household name.

Clark spent a lot of time in college developing her company. She got real-world experience working with accountants, marketers, and designers. Clark later signed with a New York sports management company.

In April 2024, Clark signed an 8-year deal with Nike. The contract is worth up to $28 million. As part of the deal, Clark gifted her Iowa teammates shoes on her twenty-second birthday, January 22, 2024.

Clark's WNBA rookie contract will pay her $338,056 over 4 years. That is much less than top NBA rookies make. One reason for this is that the NBA has more viewers. But the explosion in WNBA

Pay Gap

Fans were outraged when Clark's WNBA salary was announced. She earned $76,535 during her rookie season. The 2023 NBA's top draft pick made $12.1 million during his first year. Steph Curry makes more in one NBA game than Clark makes in 4 years. New WNBA deals are expected by 2026.

viewership is expected to greatly increase WNBA earnings.

GIVING BACK

Clark believes in helping her community. She is a philanthropist. This is a person who gives money or gifts to charity. In 2023, she started a nonprofit called the Caitlin Clark Foundation. Its mission is to empower young people and strengthen communities. The foundation focuses on helping all kids thrive.

Clark's foundation emphasizes education, nutrition, and sports. It partners with national companies such as Nike, Gatorade, and State Farm. Together, the partners raise funds and make donations. The foundation raised more than $100,000 for a local food pantry. It donated more than $35,000 to the Boys and Girls Clubs of Central Iowa.

Clark helps her community in other ways. She runs affordable basketball camps for kids. She visits children in the hospital. Clark said she was raised to go out of her way to be kind to others.

JUST THE BEGINNING

Clark wants more from her future than breaking basketball records. She wants her legacy to be the impact she can have on kids and adults. Clark says, "Never stop dreaming, because you can achieve way more than you ever thought."[8]

But Clark's drive shows that it takes more than dreaming. Already near the top of her

Caitlin Clark is shooting to be her best in all areas of her life. Through camps, hospital visits, and charitable giving, Clark works to make a difference in her community.

game, Clark still works hard to become her best, on and off the court. It's exciting to think of what her future might hold.

GLOSSARY

agents

people who represent the interests of athletes in negotiations

assists

passes to teammates that result in a score

conditioning

physical fitness

draft

the system that allows professional sports teams to choose new players each year

point guard

a player who moves the ball up the court and runs plays

recruit

to ask a player to join one's team

rookie

a person who is new at something or is in their first season

sports psychologist

a mental health professional who helps athletes improve their performance and well-being.

SOURCE NOTES

INTRODUCTION: A RECORD-SETTING SHOT

1. Quoted in Jacob Lev, Jason Hanna, and George Ramsay, "Iowa's Caitlin Clark Breaks NCAA Women's Basketball All-Time Scoring Record," *CNN*, February 16, 2024. www.cnn.com.

CHAPTER ONE: RIGHT FROM THE START

2. Quoted in Bryan Murphy, "Inside Caitlin Clark's Family Tree," *Sporting News*, May 14, 2024. www.sportingnews.com.

3. Quoted in "Caitlin Clark was a Grade-School Phenom," *Fox Sports*, February 6, 2024. www.foxsports.com.

CHAPTER TWO: IOWA HAWKEYE

4. Quoted in Wright Thompson, "Caitlin Clark and Iowa Find Peace in the Process (Part II)," *ESPN*, March 20, 2024. www.espn.com.

5. Quoted in "Caitlin Clark Wants It All: How the Iowa Star Plans to Conquer College Basketball," *Athletic*, February 17, 2022. www.nytimes.com.

CHAPTER THREE: A DREAM COME TRUE

6. Quoted in Daniel Carty, "Caitlin Clark Says She's Not Disappointed over Being Left off Olympics Team," *NBC*, June 10, 2024. www.nbc.com.

CHAPTER FOUR: MORE THAN BASKETBALL

7. Quoted in Jacqueline Tempura and Charlotte Walsh, "Meet Caitlin Clark's Family," *Women's Health*, May 14, 2024. www.womenshealthmag.com.

8. Quoted in Karl Rasmussen, "Iowa's Caitlin Clark Shares Emotional Moment with Family After Historic Night," *Sport's Illustrated*, February 15, 2024. www.si.com.

FOR FURTHER RESEARCH

BOOKS

Korey Beckett, *Caitlin Clark*. Mason Crest, 2025.

Luke Hanlon, *Caitlin Clark: Basketball Star*. Abdo, 2025.

Kristen Rajczak Nelson, *Caitlin Clark: College Basketball GOAT*. Gareth Stevens, 2025.

INTERNET SOURCES

"Caitlin Clark," *Hawkeye Sports*, 2024. www.hawkeyesports.com.

"Caitlin Clark: 2024 WNBA Rookie of the Year," *Indiana Fever*, n.d. www.fever-roty.com

Corbin McGuire. "The Caitlin Clark Effect," *NCAA*, February 15, 2024. www.ncaa.org.

WEBSITES

Caitlin Clark Foundation

http://caitlinclark22.com

The Caitlin Clark Foundation website provides information about her foundation's goal to empower youth and their families through education, nutrition, and sport. The site lists her awards and honors.

Indiana Fever

http://fever.wnba.com

The Fever's website provides links to stories and videos about the Fever and its players. Schedules and statistics are available.

WNBA

https://www.wnba.com/awardshistory

The WNBA website lists the winners of WNBA individual awards, such as MVP, Rookie of the Year, Defensive Player of the Year, and All-WNBA Teams.

INDEX

IMAGE CREDITS

Cover: © Ross D. Franklin/AP Images
5: © Erica Denhoff/Icon Sportswire
7: © Matthew Holst/Getty Images Sport/Getty Images
8: © Keith Gillett/Icon Sportswire
10: © zimmytws/Shutterstock Images
13: © Marc Piscotty/Icon Sportswire
14: © JoeSAPhotos/Shutterstock Images
19: © Luke Lu/Diamond Images/Getty Images
20: © Brocreative/Shutterstock Images
23: © Katiebtraveling/Shutterstock Images
25: © Hans Pennink/AP Images
27: © Andy Lyons/Getty Images Sport/Getty Images
31: © Maddie Meyer/Getty Images Sport/Getty Images
33: © Red Line Editorial
34: © Anton Vierietin/iStockphoto
37: © Charles Brock/Icon Sportswire
39: © Harry How/Getty Images Sport/Getty Images
41: © Joseph Denhoff/Icon Sportswire
44: © Michael Conroy/AP Images
47: © Matthew Holst/Getty Images Sport/Getty Images
49: © Dylan Buell/Getty Images Sport/Getty Images
51: © Brian Spurlock/Icon Sportswire
53: © cfg1978/Shutterstock Images
57: © Kristin Stack Hale

ABOUT THE AUTHOR

Libby Wilson never followed college or professional sports until she was captivated by Caitlin Clark's logo threes during the 2023 NCAA tournament. Since then, she has rarely missed a Clark game and has become a WNBA fan. When she's not watching women's basketball, Wilson writes books for young people. Her favorite topics include nature, history, and inspirational people. She lives in Pennsylvania and North Carolina with her husband and golden retriever.